A LITTLE BOY'S BIG DREAM

the true story of

Self-Published
By Sandy Turnbull 2025

Edited by
Flying Pants Editing
and
Julia Archer

Cover design by
Booksmith Designs

ISBN: 978-0-646-72112-5

A LITTLE BOY'S BIG DREAM

the true story of RILEY'S BIG RIDE

SANDY TURNBULL

For Riley

Table of Contents

Chapter 1 The Dream	1
Chapter 2 The Adventure Begins	5
Chapter 3 Planning	15
Chapter 4 Training Continues	22
Chapter 5 Final Preparations	30
Chapter 6 The Pandemic	34
Chapter 7 Melbourne	36
Chapter 8 Day One	40
Chapter 9 Day Two	49
Chapter 10 Day Three	55
Chapter 11 Day Four	62
Chapter 12 Day Five	67
Chapter 13 Day Six	73
Chapter 14 Life Goes On	83
Chapter 15 Riley Now	90

Chapter 1
The Dream

"Come on, Riley. Let's see what Ed's been up to," said Pop.

I climbed up onto Pop's lap to watch Ed's latest YouTube video.

Pop rides a unicycle and had found Ed's YouTube channel when searching for videos about unicycling. We had been following his journey for a few months.

Ed Pratt was a man from England with a big dream.

"Is he really going to ride a unicycle around the whole WORLD, Pop?" I asked.

"He sure is! Have a look here," Pop pulled over his world globe. "Ed lives here, in England, and he's already ridden across Europe and Asia."

"So, Australia's next?" My eyes widened.

"That's right."

The adventures Ed had experienced and the problems he had to overcome in each video were sometimes funny and at other times were a little frightening, but they always left me amazed.

Now Ed was about to arrive in Perth, Western Australia. From there he would make his way across the Nullarbor to Adelaide.

The following week, when I got to Pop's house, he greeted me with a big smile. "Guess what, Riley? Ed is coming to stay at Nan and Pop's house!"

Pop had emailed Ed and had invited him to stay. After Ed accepted the invitation, our whole family began following his journey. Via Ed's tracking device we all watched with great interest as he made his way closer to Adelaide.

My 6th birthday was in mid-August 2017. A few weeks later, on a cold, wet Sunday afternoon, Ed was approaching the town of Clare in South Australia. We put our bikes on the back of Pop's car and drove there to offer him a warm welcome. One day later, he finally made it to Nan and Pop's house.

Pop helped Ed with some repairs and getting the unicycle clean and ready for his next phase, riding to Sydney. Nan washed Ed's clothes, which hadn't been washed for some time. She'll never forget the smell!

My family and I enjoyed hearing stories about Ed's adventures and the interesting things he had gone through, firstly when planning and training for his trip, then later as his journey went on.

It was amazing to me that, even though Ed's plans had to change along the way, and his journey was not exactly how it had been planned, he completed it. With great determination and the need to not give up, Ed achieved what he had set out to do despite the obstacles he met along the way.

I was so impressed with Ed's example that I asked Pop, "Can we have an adventure like Ed?"

Pop answered, "That's a great idea! The whole world might be a bit much, though."

After thinking for a moment, I said "Let's ride to Melbourne. That would be a fantastic adventure!".

And that is how my dream began.

Meeting Ed

Pop's unicycle
Unlike a bicycle with two wheels, unicycles require a great deal of balance and coordination to ride, as riders must constantly adjust their body weight to stay upright.

Chapter 2
The Adventure Begins

Riding the whole 800 kilometres from Adelaide to Melbourne would be a great adventure, but could I really do it? I was only seven. Even though more than a year had gone by, I could not get the idea out of my head.

So, one day in March 2019, I asked Pop, "When can we ride to Melbourne?"

"Let's go to the bike shop and see if we can find a road bike small enough for you to ride," he replied.

We found the smallest road bike in the shop and adjusted its seat to the lowest position. However, even though I was quite tall for my age, I had to struggle to get my leg over the bar; I could barely touch the ground on tip toes while sitting on the seat. However, the bike was not very expensive. So, if my big adventure was not possible, Pop thought, it was not too much of a waste.

Time to make the dream real.

It was March 30th, 2019, when Pop mounted my new road bike on his trainer to teach me how to ride properly. The trainer is a kind of frame that holds the bike in place, so that you can ride it inside. The back wheel of my bike was held by the trainer and then when I mounted the bike it was just like riding on the road, except I didn't go anywhere. I just pedalled in place. That allowed me to pedal, change gears and use the brakes just as I would when riding normally. I had only ridden BMX bikes, so I had to learn a whole new riding position, how the gears worked, and – most importantly – how to use the brakes. I loved it so far.

Then it was off for our first ride together on our road bikes. Pop taught me when and why to change gears, making sure I could stop and start safely. We started from Pop's house and made our way to Gawler on the Stuart O'Grady Bike track. Then we rode all the way to the other end of the track at Port Wakefield Road, and then up the hill back to Pop's house. We rode just over 60 kilometres.

I had completed my first ride on my new road bike with a great sense of achievement! It had rained heavily, and we came back soaked, but that did not dampen my enthusiasm. I would need to get used to getting wet on a ride.

After recovering from a good first ride, Pop and I were ready to go again. The next weekend came, and I said to Pop, "Can we do one hundred kilometres today?"

"Okay, Riley," Pop said, "let's do it!"

So, on my second ever time on a road bike, I did my first 100 km ride. More specifically, we rode 107 km in 5 hours and 55 minutes. I was quickly learning that Pop and I both liked to challenge ourselves, and each other. We both loved the feeling you get when you achieve your goal.

How will I feel after riding to Melbourne? Will we succeed?

Pop had ridden bikes on and off for many years, using a bike to get to and from work. We had also done short rides together many times, but never even close to 100 km in one day.

We were both pleased with our achievement that day and Pop said, "This is just the beginning. We will need to do that many times and get a lot of miles in our legs." Pop would say that many times to me in the following months.

Even though I understood what he meant I would always say, "Don't you mean kilometres, Pop?"

We continued training regularly. On our first few rides, Pop explained to me that it was very important that I always listen to him and do exactly what he says. So, we developed signals and commands to keep ourselves as safe as possible.

Pop said, "I am like the captain of a ship; you must always follow my orders for your safety. I am responsible for you when we are out riding, and I can't let anything happen to you." I always listened hard and made sure to respond to Pop's commands.

On each ride we were finding the roads to try and avoid and where the best route was to safely reach our destination for the day. When possible, we would ride on bike tracks until we needed to hit the road. We soon discovered that Adelaide was very inconsistent with bike lanes. These lanes would start and end with what seemed no reason. Not all roads had a good shoulder either. The shoulder is the bitumen on the left of the solid white line.

The shoulders can be as good as the road or at times full of potholes, very rough or non-existent.

My parents were always a bit nervous when we were out for hours at a time on the roads. They were then relieved when they heard that we had arrived home safely and wanted to know about our day and how far we had ridden.

This early training was vital; I had much to learn. For example, I learnt the hard way that I had to drink plenty of water to avoid cramping up. Cramp in the legs is not good, especially when you are riding. Before leaving on a ride Pop would always say, "Riley, have you had a big glass of water?"

"Yes, Pop," I would answer, as I quickly ran back inside for the drink I had forgotten.

I also learnt that I had to eat lots of food. If you don't eat enough, you run out of energy quickly, and it gets very hard to keep your legs pushing. It is almost as if your legs are very heavy and made of jelly.

Another lesson was about distance. Never ride too close to the bike in front, because otherwise you could clip the rear wheel of the bike in front. If that happens, you lose balance and come off your bike and hit the ground. Yes, I learned that one the hard way, too. One day, as we were on the bike track, I lost concentration for a moment and hit the ground hard. Luckily, I came away with just a few grazes, but my bike got its first scratches. They were not the last, though.

Hardly a weekend went by when Pop and I didn't get on our bikes and ride at least 100 km. When time allowed, there would be two rides on a weekend. I was feeling great.

Nan and Pop now believed that the dream was more than a wish: I was serious about riding to Melbourne. People started to ask how our training was progressing, so Nan decided to track our riding and post the information on the Internet. My Aunty Meg designed a logo and helped Nan to setup the blog and a bit later our Facebook page. See *rileysbigride.home.blog and Riley's Big Ride on Facebook*.

Friday nights I would often sleep at Nan and Pop's house so we could be up and off early. We stuffed the pockets of our jerseys with muesli bars, a spare tube in case of a flat tyre and a cylinder to inflate the tyre. Whenever we got a puncture, Pop was very quick at replacing the tube and getting us back on the road. The most important thing in Pop's pocket, of course, was our lunch money. After Pop checked the weather, wind speed and wind direction, we were ready for the day's ride.

I also love football. When the season began that year, I was playing in an Under Eights team in the Adelaide Plains football competition. Our games were played in different locations stretching from Virginia in Adelaide, all the way to Port Wakefield.

Pop, with our bikes and gear already loaded in his car, would come along to watch each game. After the game, we ate a snack, then got on the bikes. Each ride usually clocked up at least 100 km.

Many of our games were played in country towns such as Balaklava, Mallala, and Hamley Bridge, so we enjoyed riding on quiet country roads with attractive farmland for us to admire. Pop often asked, "Riley do you know what that crop is?" or explained different kinds of farm machinery. I had often wondered what those huge sprinkler looking things in the middle of paddocks were, it turns out that they are centre pivots. Pop explained that farmers use them to water their paddocks, but they can also be used with fertilizer or sometimes with weed spray. They can be set to whatever speed the farmer requires. Just as the name suggests, they pivot from the centre and move around to cover a big area saving a lot of time for the farmer. There was always something interesting to see or learn about.

In June 2019 we completed our first 150 km ride. We left early from my home in Virginia. The ride would take Pop and me into the city, and then down to Glenelg, along the coast to Semaphore and back home. As we approached home, I realised that our distance was 147 km, so I called out to Pop, "We need to add another 3 km!"

Pop looked down at his phone and yelled back at me, "YES, we sure do." So, we turned around and rode around the block; no way was I stopping so close to 150 km. I felt such a sense of achievement that I was excited to get inside and let everyone know about our day.

I continued to get more followers on the blog and Facebook. People were so encouraging and supportive. I especially enjoyed arriving at school on Monday mornings, so I could talk to my Principal Illia.

He is a cyclist, too, so he would ask me, "How far did you ride on the weekend? Tell me all about it." We would talk about my distance and average speed, and he would always encourage me to keep going.

It wasn't always easy, but I was determined to keep going and improve my stamina. I pushed a little harder with each ride, always keeping track of our distance and average speed on my bike computer.

It was a whole new riding experience when I was fitted with riding shoes and cleats. These allowed me to clip my shoes into the pedals, which makes riding much more efficient, as I not only push down on the pedals but also pull up. Learning to clip in and out as the bike stops and starts was quite easy and didn't cause any problems, and I enjoyed the extra power I could get. I was determined to get this right, because I had seen a few times when riders had pulled up at traffic lights and didn't unclip fast enough. They had fallen sideways and hit the ground with their shoes still clipped in. This wasn't going to happen to me.

We celebrated each new achievement, becoming more and more convinced that my dream could become reality. Planning began, and by the time I had my 8th birthday we had been training for about four and a half months. During this time, I had already done seven rides of over 100 km, clocking up over 1,500 km in total, at an average of just over 20 km/h.

Taking a break in Glenelg

Riding home from football

Leaving home excited for a big ride

A good wide shoulder

A bad shoulder with no bitumen

Chapter 3
Planning

While the training continued planning got underway, Pop spent hours looking at maps and trying to find the safest route between Adelaide and Melbourne.

Pop was discussing with Mum and Dad about our route and safety when Mum said, "Can we change the ride to start in Melbourne and finish in Adelaide?"

"That's a great idea," said Pop

Mum replied with excitement, "I think it would be great because we could have a big celebration when you reach Adelaide and invite people to the finish line."

Dad then asked, "I wonder if we could have someone to drive behind the riders to warn the traffic that there is a kid on a bike and keep you both safe, especially on the highway?"

"That's a great idea! I would feel much better knowing we would have some protection, especially for

Riley's safety." Thinking for a moment, Pop answered, "I know who the perfect person would be -- Peter."

"Yes, he would be the perfect person," said Mum.

Peter, my mum's boss at the time who we had known for many years, is an experienced driver. A long time Country Fire Service volunteer, he had been driving fire trucks and was involved in training young volunteers.

Mum and Pop went to see Peter the next week. Pop said, "Peter, I know you have been following Riley's Big Ride on social media. We are wondering if you would like to be involved?"

"I have been following with great interest and would love to be involved. What do you have in mind?".

"We have decided that for Riley's safety that we would like to have a car following to warn other traffic that we are on the road. We feel that of all the people we know you would be the most capable."

After pausing for a moment, he answered, "Yes, I could do that, it's a good idea. I will have to put some thought into how this would work, but I would love to help."

"Thank you," said Mum, "I feel much better now knowing Riley will have some protection."

Peter, together with Pop, helped over the next few months to finalise the route and make sure that it would cover exactly 800 km. Peter came up with safety protocols to keep us safe on the road. It was going to be a big responsibility for him.

I was thinking about how Ed the unicyclist had raised money for a charity called School in a Bag during his trip. They provide backpacks filled with school supplies to poor and vulnerable children throughout the world and thought I could do something like that.

"Mum," I said, "can we raise money like Ed did?"

"Great idea! Who do you think we could support?"

"I would like to help sick kids."

"We can get Nan to help you do some research into charities."

Nan did some research and after explaining to me the work done by some local charities, I decided that I would like to help the Little Heroes Foundation (LHF).

A meeting was set up with Chris McDermott the CEO and ex Adelaide Crows player, Anna Meares, an Australian cycling hero and ambassador at LHF, and Jan who would be our main contact at the charity.

Like most people we had approached there was some doubt that an eight-year-old could ride from Melbourne to Adelaide.

Chris said, "I am a little concerned that this idea is far too dangerous."

Pop replied, "We are taking every measure to keep both Riley and me safe and will have a safety car following."

Anna said, "Riley you will only be eight years old, do you really think you can ride that far?"

"Yes, I have been training hard and really will do my best to get it done," I said.

"I am impressed that at your age you're willing to give it a go," Chris said.

"We are training hard and believe that it can be done," was Pop's reply. "But we will not continue if we believe that Riley is at any risk."

After further discussion, and a promise from Pop that if was not safe for me that we would not continue, it was agreed that we would work together. It was at this meeting that we came up with the slogan

8 years old
8 days
800 km
$8000

Peter volunteered his business ICL to become a sponsor by donating magnetic signs for our cars displaying my logo and the Little Heroes Foundation, as well as giving his time to join us on the ride. Now we had our first two sponsors with Meg from Meg Shephard Designs helping with logos and social media.

Mum and Nan worked hard, sending letters and emails with details of our rides so far. Pop kept a spreadsheet of all our rides and our plans for the ride and these were sent to bike stores and manufactures and other businesses to try and secure sponsorships, mostly with no answer or a negative response.

We were lucky enough by the end of 2019 to receive from 99 Bikes some helmets, tyres and tubes.

Pop's boss Bruce at HVG agreed to provide our custom kits. Mum designed our jerseys and knicks with my logo, sponsors and the Little Heroes Foundation proudly displayed in bright blue and yellow so that we would be easily seen on the road. When they arrived in early 2020, we thought we really looked the part.

I didn't know that Nan had had a reply from Sola Sport, the agent for a bike company called Bianchi Australia at the time to say that our new bikes were on the way.

Now a start date needed to be decided. It was important to find a time of the year when the weather would be at its best and there were no public or school holidays so there would be a little less traffic on the road. March 22nd, 2020 was to be our start date, with our schedule organised to secure accommodation and so that I was clear in my mind what each day's distance would be.

A rest day was included in Bordertown near Pop's hometown where we had arranged some fundraising events and a visit to Mundulla Primary School that Pop had attended as a child. We would arrive back in Adelaide on March 30th, 2020, exactly one year since my first ride on a road bike.

More letters and emails were sent, and our accommodation was booked in most cases at a discount or donation to the Little Heroes Foundation.

Our planned itinerary:

Sunday March 22
Day 1 Melbourne (Docklands) to Ballarat 111 km

Monday March 23
Day 2 Ballarat to St Arnaud 132 km

Tuesday March 24
Day 3 St Arnaud to Warracknabeal 98 km

Wednesday March 25
Day 4 Warracknabeal to Nhill 89 km

Thursday March 26
Day 5 Nhill to Bordertown 86 km

Friday March 27
Day off Mundulla
Visit Mundulla Primary School
Visit Turnbull Farm
Visit Mundulla Church of Christ
Visit Bordertown Classic Car Club

Saturday March 28
Day 6 Bordertown to Coonalpyn 112 km

Sunday March 29
Day 7 Coonalpyn to Kanmantoo 115 km

Monday March 30
Day 8 Kanmantoo to Adelaide Oval 57 km

Meeting Chris McDermott and Anna Meares

Chapter 4
Training Continues

In December 2019 much to my surprise two new bikes from Bianchi Australia arrived. It was the evening of my end of year school concert. When we got home Pop said, "Come out here Riley," as he walked out of the back door to the carport.

"Where are we going Pop?" I said, following him with my family close behind.

"Look at these Riley," he said, as he stood in front of two shiny new bikes.

"Wow! Where did they come from?" I asked with my eyes wide open.

"We have a new sponsor, Bianchi Australia. Don't they look great?"

"They sure do! Can we go for a ride?"

"Tomorrow mate, it's a bit late now."

I thought they were the best-looking bikes I had ever seen and couldn't wait for morning to come. Waking up the next morning I felt excited about our new bikes. We left early for another 100 km ride. I found the new bike much lighter and enjoyed the extra speed I could get and felt proud on my new bike.

Another lesson learnt was in January 2020 when together Pop and I completed our first 200 km ride in 8 hours and 19 minutes -- saddle sores! I am sure most cyclist know about saddle sores, but if you don't, just imagine every part of your body that touches the seat with a very painful, very red, rash.

It had been difficult to get well-fitting bike knicks for me which didn't help that day. Knicks are the lycra shorts that cyclist wear; they have padding in the crotch to protect your butt from the hard seat that road bikes have and are tight fitting to avoid movement that causes friction. It took a few days for my butt to recover! It was painful to even sit down, so a few weeks later when the kits that HVG had had made for us arrived, it was much more comfortable. Also, the newly acquired butt cream used to prevent friction on long days riding meant no more saddle sores for me.

Our rides often ended in Virginia where I lived. There is a small dog in a yard on the way home and I knew that every time we rode past that little dog would race out and try to nip my heels. Pop thought it was amusing and as we got close, he would call out, "Are you ready?"

No matter how far we had ridden that day I would find the energy to put on the afterburners so that little dog couldn't keep up and thankfully never got the satisfaction of it nipping my heels.

Magpies also became another reason for me to put on the afterburners. There really is no way to outrun a swooping magpie, but I still try to this day! We began to know in the springtime where we would come across a swooping magpie. I would get down low and go as fast as I could, but both Pop and I have felt the peck of a magpie on our helmets and the pain when they peck the back of your neck.

The weather is something that can't be controlled, so during our training, Pop and I endured freezing mornings when our fingers and toes were numb. Rain, heat and all kinds of wind, there were not many days when a ride was cancelled due to the weather.

A quick check of the forecast would determine where we would ride that day. And then I would always ask the question, "Where will we have lunch today, Pop?"

If it was going to be windy then we would start the day into the wind so the ride home would benefit from a tail wind behind us. On very hot days it would be an early start to try and be home before it became too hot. Keeping the water bottles filled, especially on those hot days, was important and I enjoyed it when we would stop and ask at a McDonalds for some water and our bottles would be filled with ice and water by the staff.

When it was a very hot day, we would find a petrol station with an outside tap and put our heads under the tap to cool off.

Hills, oh those hills. I did not enjoy getting up those hills! Even though I never enjoyed the hills, I knew it was an important part of our training and Pop would always say, "What goes up must come down".

I always struggled to keep up with Pop when riding up hills and would hear him yelling out, "Come on Riley push hard we will be at the top soon," encouraging me to keep going.

Coming downhill it is easy to go very fast with no effort at all, but Pop had made a rule that 60 km/h was to be our limit for my safety. We would often need to brake hard squeezing the brake levers constantly to slow ourselves down, watching our speed while concentrating on the road ahead.

Pop had a bad accident years ago, one day when riding home from work. It was when he was trying to go as fast as he could down a steep hill. He hit a plate on the road and went headfirst over his handlebars, cracking his helmet and leaving him with a gash to his head, a broken collar bone and badly grazed arms and legs.

There was no way he was going to allow that to happen to me! So, we were very sure always to be extra careful coming downhill.

As the weeks and months went on, both Pop and I were getting fitter and stronger. After riding more than 100 km I would get home and go out and kick the football or run around with my brother and sister. There was no stopping me.

There were a few people during our training that Mum was approached by who criticised and accused her of forcing me to do so much riding and endangering my health with too much exercise. This was beginning to upset Mum, so she took me to the doctor and explained about my Big Ride. She asked if at my age it was going to have any effect on my health.

The doctor asked me, "Are you being forced to ride or using any energy supplements?"

I answered her, "No! It was my idea and I love it, and we keep our energy up by eating regularly and drinking lots of water."

The doctor looked at me, and then at Mum, and said, much to Mum's relief, "I can't see that a young person exercising and working towards a goal is bad for them in any way. I would like to wish you luck and would love to see more young people working hard for something."

We left the doctor's office feeling better. Mum was now ready with a reply for the next person that questioned her!

Training had taken Pop and me all around Adelaide and surrounding towns. It wasn't unusual that while sitting and eating lunch for someone to recognise me or notice I was a young boy and come over for a chat about the day's ride, often surprised at my age and the distance we were riding that day.

I carried some business cards that we had made with the web address for my blog and Facebook page and proudly handed them out when talking to anyone who was interested. I had been too shy when we first began riding to talk to people, but with my confidence growing, I was beginning to enjoy talking to people and explaining about my Big Ride.

I also enjoyed it when another cyclist would ride alongside us for a while and have a chat or yell out to me.

"Keep going young fella."

Or when I was recognised and hear, "It's the Bianchi boys."

Motorist were not always so kind and would occasionally yell out and abuse us as they passed. We had a few times had rubbish or a drink bottle thrown at us from car windows. I was hit on the helmet by a bag of rubbish one day, but we didn't let that worry us too much.

It was special to spend so much time with my Pop every weekend, an experience I will never forget. He taught me many things; we visited lots of places and of course had some great lunches.

Loving our new bikes

Looking good in our new kits

Chapter 5
Final Preparations

March was fast approaching and as the training continued final preparations were being made. Together Pop and Peter decided what spare parts and equipment would be needed in case of break downs for the bikes and these were acquired.

Peter developed safety signals, acquired flashing lights for the top of his Ute and walkie talkies, Pop would carry one in the pocket of his jersey. If anything was needed Peter could communicate with him using these and there was no need for us to carry snacks or a spare tube. A much more detailed schedule was formalised to include breaks to refill water bottles, morning tea and lunch.

Fundraising was well underway and early in March a local hotel offered to hold a schnitzel night where they would donate $5 for every schnitzel sold. It was a great night with about 100 people attending: family, friends, schoolteachers and even some people who had been following our social media. We also had some great donations for a raffle and that night raised a little more than $1500 for LHF, it was a great night and great to have so much encouraging support.

Mum had contacted some local TV channels and radio stations to see if they would be interested in hearing my story. Channel 10 Adelaide replied, and the reporter Taylor Ryan and her cameraman came to Nan and Pop's house and interviewed us.

I was very nervous with that big camera pointing at me and having to answer so many questions. After the interview they asked us to kit up and ride around a bit as we were being filmed. The story was aired on the news the next night. It was an interesting experience for me, and it was exciting to see myself on the news.

Bec, a journalist from our local paper The Two Wells Echo, interviewed me and the story was on the front page. It was great exposure and even though it felt a little nerve wracking, the story helped get the fundraising goal moving up and we gained more followers on social media.

Pop had arranged with the South Australia Police traffic division for a Police escort to accompany us for the last few kilometres into Adelaide oval and Taylor from Channel 10 was booked to cover the end of the ride. Friends, family and supporters were ready to follow each day's ride and gather at the Adelaide Oval for the big finish.

It was just days before our departure and while all of this was going on the bikes were serviced, cleaned and we did a final check to make sure that we had everything we may need.

Pop had a call from George the Bianchi Australia importer who offered more support. George arranged that on our arrival in Melbourne we would go to a local Bianchi dealer and anything we needed would be available to us at no cost. This was unexpected as we already had been supported so well by Bianchi Australia!

Bags were packed, the bikes were loaded on the car and goodbyes were said to family and friends and my younger brother and sister, Toby and Dakota, were left with family.

I was pleased that my fundraising was going well and had already reached about $4,500 of our $8000 goal and I enjoyed the feeling that each time I checked there had been more donations.

Finally, after so much planning and training it was time for my adventure to begin.

Being interviewed for the news

Chapter 6
The Pandemic

As we were making our final preparations, news of COVID-19 started to appear from overseas. It was interesting as we heard that this disease had spread from China and was beginning to appear in America and Europe. Those places were so far from Australia so there was nothing to be too worried about, we thought.

Then on March 11th, 2020, the World Health Organisation declared COVID-19 a Global Pandemic. I had no idea what a Global Pandemic was. It didn't seem very important to me, and I didn't know how we might be affected.

There had only been a few COVID-19 cases in Australia; some people had brought it from overseas. The Government had forced them to isolate in hotels to make sure, that they couldn't infect anyone, hoping that they could control the spread of the disease.

I was very excited that my great grandparents were going to arrive from New Zealand and would be in Melbourne to see the start of the ride, then travel to Adelaide to cheer us over the finish line. But just days before they were due to arrive, international borders were closed. Flights were cancelled, and sadly they would have to just follow our ride from New Zealand. We were disappointed, but what could we do?

Social distancing was introduced. We were told to keep 1.5 metres away from other people and to use hand sanitiser and wash our hands regularly. The shops had signs everywhere, reminding us how far apart to stand. It was very strange!

Perhaps the strangest thing was the shortage of toilet paper. People had been buying up all the toilet paper and leaving the shelves empty. The TV news was showing people physically fighting in supermarkets over packets. Was the world going mad?

As we were preparing to leave for Melbourne, COVID-19 was spreading a bit more, but at this stage with hand washing and social distancing it was not looking too bad. We were all sure that we would be fine. Scott Morrison, the Prime Minister, had been having frequent press conferences keeping everyone updated daily and we would be following the news closely.

What would this mean for our ride?

Chapter 7
Melbourne

I travelled to Melbourne full of excitement and nerves in the car with my parents and arrived in Melbourne on Friday evening the 20th of March. We were going to attend the Arnold Classic Strong Man show on Saturday. When we arrived in Melbourne it was announced that the show was cancelled due to COVID-19. Disappointed, we spent the morning walking around the streets waiting for the rest of the crew to arrive.

Nan and Pop arrived early in the afternoon with the bikes and all the necessary gear. They had a banner with my logo and all our sponsors listed to hang up at our stops to promote the ride and help with fundraising loaded in their car.

After settling into the hotel and unloading all the gear we set off to the bike shop that Bianchi Australia had organised for us to visit, and I was amazed that we were able to choose whatever we wanted at no cost. We were careful to not take too much and be seen as greedy, so with some new water bottles, hats, saddle bags, tires and tubes, we left the store feeling great.

As we walked around the streets after leaving what seemed a relatively normal Adelaide, the Melbourne Docklands, usually full of people on a Saturday afternoon, was quiet and some of the shops were closed while others were only allowing a few people inside at a time. Some people were wearing face masks, and I thought they looked ridiculous.

Late in the afternoon Peter arrived in his big red Ute. It was getting exciting now everyone was here, and tomorrow was the big day. Peter's Ute which was already stocked with a big water container to keep our bottles filled, first aid kit and a bag of snacks for the riders was loaded with the bike spare parts.

The cars were looking great with the *Riley's Big Ride* magnetic signs on the doors. Dad's car fridge was loaded with supplies for morning teas and lunches in the back of his 4WD.

Peter would follow behind the bikes with flashing lights on top of his Ute. Mum and Dad were in their car and Nan was in another car, making up our roadside crew. They would go ahead to the next spot that had been organised and set up ready for us to take a break.

Together we walked to the exact spot out the front of Marvel Stadium where the ride would start in the morning. This was what we had been working so hard for and dreaming about for so long. I was feeling nervous and wondering: could I really ride all the way back to Adelaide?

Pop said, "This is it Riley, your big dream is about to come true, are you excited?"

"I can't believe it we are here; this is going to be so much fun!"

Trying to find somewhere for our evening meal, we saw that many of the restaurants were offering half price meals because they were wanting to use up their supplies, not knowing if the Government might force them to close. While enjoying the meal, Peter went through the safety signals again.

Peter took his role of safety officer seriously and said, "If at any time I think that Pop or you are unable to continue, or if you are at any risk, I will call the ride off because when you asked me to do this your safety became my responsibility." We agreed.

It was hard to believe that after 6070 kilometres and 274 hours of training, almost one year and many, many of hours of planning and dreaming, tomorrow we would begin! My Big Ride would no longer be a dream but a reality.

With a plan to meet at the start line at 7.30 in the morning for an 8 o'clock start, we said goodnight and headed back to the hotel for an early night.

Checking out tomorrow's start

Chapter 8
Day One

Sunday 22nd of March 2020
Melbourne Docklands – Ballarat

After a good night's sleep and a big breakfast prepared by Mum, I went to Nan and Pop's hotel room to get ready. Putting on my riding gear I felt very excited and talked to Pop about how my dream had begun. Pop said to me once again, "Today will be the toughest day of the ride, getting up the hill to Ballarat. We have done so much hard work for this day, and we will need to push hard."

I wasn't sure if I was feeling nervous or if it was excitement, but my heart seemed to be beating very fast, and I just wanted to get going. All dressed, we did a quick check to make sure the bikes were in good order and finally, we were ready to go.

Pop and I wheeled our bikes out of the hotel room and down the lift carrying our helmets and shoes. It was just a few minutes' walk to the start line and the excitement was building.

There was hardly a car to be seen, and no one was out for a morning walk. It was very strange for Melbourne to seem so deserted.

It was a cold morning but the emotions we were feeling didn't allow us to worry about the temperature.

Peter arrived with lights flashing on top of his freshly washed Ute and pulled up on the footpath next to us.

A few last-minute instructions from Peter, some photos, and words of encouragement from everyone, then Pop and I mounted our bikes and clipped our shoes in. This was it, we were really going to do it, riding all the way back to Adelaide!

Full of excitement and a little nervous with Peter following behind lights flashing, we started the ride towards Ballarat, with the cheers of my parents and Nan echoing in the distance as we left them at the start line.

As I pedalled alongside Pop heading out of the city, thinking about how amazing it was that our ride had begun, the crew returned to the hotel, packed up their cars and headed to the very first scheduled stop, BP at Rockbank.

Pop and I made our way out of Melbourne towards the Western Highway, while the crew enjoyed a warm coffee inside out of the cold, waiting for our very first stop and wondering if I was feeling alright. We arrived for a quick stop for a snack and a water bottle check, and Mum said, "I am surprised that you are already here, that was quick! Are you feeling, okay Riley?"

"Yes, I am good. We are pushing hard this morning to keep our speed up before we get to the hill."

We were off again. It was still cold, and light rain began falling as we made our way to Bacchus Marsh where we turned off the freeway for a stop. It was a quick stop for a regroup and water bottles were filled. I was feeling great and ready to go with Pop's words in my head, "Here comes the hill."

The hard part of the day's ride was about to begin. The climb up the Pentland Hills to Ballan meant about 21 km of climbing. The rain continued as Pop and I pushed up the hill, my legs burning and struggling to suck in enough air. I thought, "Will this hill ever end?" It seemed to be endless. Why did I ever think I could do this?

While we kept pushing upwards, I was looking for the top of the hill, but each time we turned a bend I could see it was still going and each time my heart sank a little.

In their cars the crew were listening to the news as things began to change. Weddings and funerals had been capped at ten people a few days ago, and now restaurants and hotels were closed and could only serve takeaway.

Pop and I continued to struggle up the hill. When at last we arrived in Ballan cold, wet and exhausted I was wondering why I had thought this was going to be fun. I was not enjoying day one. I knew it was going to be hard, but not this hard.

Mum said, "Sorry guys they have just announced new COVID rules. You will have to wait out here while I go in and get your food." We had to stay outside in the cold and rain to eat!

Pop and I were feeling exhausted, I had tears rolling down my cheeks wondering what was going to happen next with COVID. It seemed that every time we stopped the rules would change and it was too much for me to think about.

I was beginning to wonder if I could complete this ride. That hill had been harder than any other ride I had experienced. It was pure determination that kept my legs going when each turn of my pedals was getting harder, and my legs were burning, but my mind would not let me give up.

Mum asked, "Are you okay to keep going Riley?"

I answered "Yes, that was really hard." But I wasn't sure.

"Only 36 km to go then we will be in Ballarat." Pop said. "The worst of the hills are done, and the last 5 km will be downhill." I was relieved to hear that, so we set off wet and feeling exhausted.

The crew went ahead and made their way to Ballarat to buy supplies for the evening meal and were surprised to find the supermarket shelves were stripped bare of a lot of essentials. Then they made their way to check into the accommodation.

Once checked in, the crew went out on the street to await our arrival, unaware that for the last 20 kms of the ride into Ballarat Pop had been suffering with cramps in his legs and we had to stop a few times for him to stretch. They were surprised when Pop come around the corner walking his bike with me riding slowly alongside him.

It had been just before the corner when Pop got off his bike with another cramp and couldn't get his leg back over the bike.

We walked to our cabin and Pop sat down while Nan removed his shoes because he couldn't raise his legs to do it himself!

I enjoyed a nice warm shower and Pop rested. While the evening meal was being prepared, I was excited to find a pool and even though it was cold I jumped in, but finding it was far too cold, I quickly hopped out realising that it was not a good idea. I played for a while on the jumping pillow and then rode around the park on a pedal cart with Peter as my passenger. Everyone was surprised that I still seemed to have plenty of energy left but I was feeling great with those hills behind me.

After the meal as the day's achievement was being celebrated, we were all feeling good about the next few days, especially now that we had those hills behind us. We crowded around to hear South Australia's Premier, Steven Marshall's press conference on Mum's phone.

The news he delivered was unexpected and quickly changed our mood. He gave the direction that South Australia's border with Victoria would be closed at 4 pm on Tuesday 24th March. The direction stated that after the specified time anyone who crossed the border would have to return immediately to their home and spend 14 days in isolation.

We were due to cross the border on Thursday 26th. Suddenly our excitement about today's achievement, Pop and I completing that tough ride, turned into thoughts about what to do next.

Pop said, "What should we do now? We could ride straight for the border, but I am not sure we could make it in time."

"It could be done, but I think we might run out of time. It's a bit risky and we may not be able to get there before 4 pm," Peter answered.

"I am not ready to give up. Are you, Riley?" said Pop.

"No," I said, "but I don't know what we can do."

"We might not have any choice. Let's see what we can work out," said Mum.

The maps came out. How could we get to the border before that time? What would we be required to do? Should we just pack up in the morning and drive home?

After much debate and phone calls with family at home it was decided that giving up and going home was not really an option for us yet. Somehow, we needed to get to Nhill by tomorrow night, 260 km away from Ballarat then cross the border earlier than the required time and decide what we would be able to do next.

Mum phoned our next two nights' accommodation to cancel our booking and changed our arrival in Nhill to Monday evening instead of Wednesday. We were relieved when that was sorted out.

With disappointment that our carefully put together plans were no longer, everyone went to bed early, unsure of what would come next. We had prepared for everything or so we thought; breakdowns, injuries, bad weather but not what COVID-19 would throw us.

I went to bed not really knowing what was going to happen, feeling confused and a little bit scared.

112 km 5 hours Average 22.4 km/h

Distance
112.01 km

Elevation Gain
1,103 m

Moving Time
5:00:35

Avg Speed
22.4 km/h

Max Elevation
617 m

Max Speed
50.8 km/h

Excited for day 1

Ready to go with my banner

Peter's Ute ready to keep us safe

Chapter 9
Day Two

Monday 23rd of March 2020
Ballarat – Stawell (Nhill)

Overnight Pop was disappointed but not surprised, to receive messages cancelling our fundraising events in Bordertown and our visit to Mundulla Primary School.

With our new route for today sorted out everyone was ready to go except for me. I refused to get out of bed because yesterday's news that changed all our plans had hit me hard. I couldn't understand why this was happening. It was scary, and I just wanted to go home. If Pop couldn't even finish on his bike yesterday, how was I going to do this? It was the first time I had really doubted that I could do this.

Nan came into the cabin and said, "Let's get going Riley. Let's make the next two days fun. Don't worry anymore, whatever happens when we reach the border we will deal with when we get there."

"What if they don't let us finish when we get to the border?" I said, thinking about the people that were following and not wanting to let them down by not finishing.

"If that's what happens we will all be very disappointed, but we will just have to do what we are told. No one will blame you, Riley."

"Okay. I will try to forget about COVID."

I got out of bed and ate a quick breakfast. Feeling a bit happier, I got myself ready for the day, determined to just have fun.

Leaving Ballarat, Pop's legs were still bothering him, but they were feeling a bit better after a good rest, and I was now excited for today's ride.

We rode out of the park while the crew packed up and drove ahead to our first scheduled break. It was very cold as we rode along, but the scenery was nice with lots of trees and rolling hills. There was not a lot of traffic and when we saw the crew waiting for us near Carngham with a snack it felt good to get off the bike. It was so cold that Mum gave me my dressing gown to keep me warm while Peter filled our water bottles, and we had a snack. Pop's phone rang while we were having a break. It was the Head of the South Australian Police Traffic Division to inform us that we would no longer get a police escort into Adelaide Oval, and we would need to cross the border into South Australia as soon as possible and follow directions given to us when we did so.

We were off riding again and trying to put everything COVID out of our minds. Riding through Trawalla Forest was probably our favourite part of the whole trip. More great scenery and we felt like we were flying along with a fresh tail wind helping us along, riding two abreast.

It was calm and peaceful, such a contrast to the day before when we were riding on the noisy Western Freeway. As we were going along at speed down a hill and coming around a bend, we spotted the crew who had set up for a break and we reluctantly pulled over to join them. I was just wanting to keep riding. But I knew we had to eat to keep our energy up.

We sat down, and once again. I put on my dressing gown and Pop had a rug to keep his legs warm while Peter, as he did at every break, made sure our water bottles were filled. Pop was making sure now to drink more than he usually did to try and keep from cramping up again and, as we did at each stop, we handed the hand sanitiser around and Peter wiped the door handles of each car with disinfectant wipes.

I was keen to get going, I was having a great time and doing my best to forget about COVID and just enjoy riding.

A few kilometres and we were back on the Western Highway, not far from Beaufort. It was a new section of the highway with a wide and very smooth shoulder which made riding easy. Riding single file with Peter behind, lights flashing to warn motorist that we were there, with one wheel on the shoulder and the other on the road. Pop was telling me to look at the mountains on our right and excitedly told me all about Mount Buangor which is the highest peak in the area and Pop pointed out the huge wind farm.

We pulled into a parking bay off the highway and met the crew who had our lunch, sandwiches, and cake ready for us. It had warmed up a little by now and I was feeling good really enjoying the ride, but Pop was still struggling a bit with his legs that had not quite recovered from yesterday. Thankfully not cramping up. We got back in the saddle and rode through to Langig Gharin State Park with some ups and downs and more great scenery, and we even spotted an eagle circling above us! We were making good speed on the still-smooth road with the wind behind us. Great Western was our next stop where the crew had hung our banner on a tree. A quick snack and water bottle refresh and off again towards our final stop in Stawell

Arriving in Stawell, everyone was feeling sad that we had to load the bikes onto Pop's car. The night before, we had decided that Stawell would be the end of our ride for the day.

We drove to Nhill to make sure we could cross the border before the cut off time that the Government had set. It was such a disappointment, and the drive was silent as we should have been riding, but it was not possible to make it across the border in time. If only we had one more day, it could have been done.

When we arrived at the Caravan Park, we were surprised to see so many people as the night before in Ballarat the park was almost empty. It turned out that most of the other people were also South Australians wanting to cross the border tomorrow, making sure to do so before the cut off at 4 pm.

Although there were a lot of people around everybody was keeping their distance and not mingling.

We had dinner still feeling disappointed that we had not ridden our bikes for the last bit of today. I was thinking about Ed's unicycle journey and how he had to change his plans. Just like him, we couldn't control everything. We had an early night wondering what would happen at the border tomorrow. Would we be forced to pack up and drive home? Could we add to our ride in South Australia or just ride home as quickly as possible?

130 km 4 hours 37 minutes Average 28.1 km/h

Distance
130.05 km

Elevation Gain
806 m

Moving Time
4:37:41

Avg Speed
28.1 km/h

Max Elevation
470 m

Max Speed
58.3 km/h

Keeping warm

Chapter 10
Day Three
Tuesday 24th March 2020
Nhill – Bordertown

Waking up on this morning, everyone was feeling a little anxious. Today we would cross the border and find out if we could continue our ride or not. The reality that we may be sent straight home was heartbreaking for me and all the crew. So much effort with planning and the hours of training to prepare -- was it all going to be wasted?

I was ready to go, but Pop was dragging his feet a little. While I was waiting, I rode around the park again and again, as fast as I could, over the speed humps. The crew were telling me to save my energy, but I just kept doing laps. A few people were packing up getting ready to leave and were cheering me on as they had realised from the signs on the cars what we were doing and some of them had looked up the blog and made donations.

Pop was ready now and we rode out of the park. Pop was still struggling a little with his legs and I was full of nerves about what today would bring when we finally made it to the border.

It was a bit warmer this morning. Nhill is 64 km from the border, so to add a few kilometres and avoid traffic heading for the border on the highway we rode out west on a country road through a small town, Miram and headed back onto the highway towards Kaniva. We passed a few dead kangaroos who had been stuck by trucks. One of these was rotten and the smell was overwhelming and almost made me vomit.

We had a break in Kaniva at a playground and Pop's Auntie Mary came to see us. I had fun for a while on the playground, enjoying the day as much as I could.

Next stop: the border, 25 km away. The crew went ahead, and we all were wondering what would happen next. Was my dream going to be over in just a few kilometres' time?

The crew arrived at the border to see five police cars assembled. Dad went over and spoke to the officers about my ride. Feeling a bit confused about what we were required to do, Dad was thrilled when the police told him that because we would cross before the cut of time of 4 pm we could continue heading towards Adelaide in our own time.

Pop and I were still riding with Peter behind us not knowing yet that we were able to continue.

A few kilometres before we reached the border Pop pulled out wide and motioned me to come alongside him and he said, "Take the lead Riley and cross the border first."

I went to the front and pushed hard knowing this may be the end of our ride. It was just before 11 am and seeing the border just ahead was exciting. As I pulled into the parking bay, my heart beating fast, I crossed the line on the ground as fast as I could and for the first time ever, I had trouble unclipping my shoes and hit the ground hard. No harm was done, but I did hear some giggles and felt a little embarrassed so I jumped up to my feet as quickly as I could.

Dad excitedly said, "I explained to the police what we are doing, and they told me that we can continue and make our way home in our own time."

We were all very excited. It was decided that we should check and call the Police Sargent at the traffic control who had called Pop yesterday just to check. We didn't want to do the wrong thing and were pleased when he agreed that we could continue. We quickly made some phone calls to family at home with the news.

What is a border? Just a line on a map is what I had always thought, but I was learning its more than just a line! Different Governments with different rules, different speed limits and now different COVID restrictions and, as we were about to find out, different roads.

We now had a whole new burst of enthusiasm. The mood of the whole crew had changed. "Let's get going, Pop," I said as we got back on our bikes with excitement and a plan to meet the crew in Bordertown at the bakery.

I was full of energy and never so happy to be on my bike.

It was surprising after the great shoulders we had ridden on in Victoria that in South Australia the shoulder was rough and made us feel like we were riding on cobblestones!

Pop was still having some trouble with his legs and had been leading for almost the whole trip so far, but he asked me to lead the rest of the way today to give him a bit of a break. It is always harder being the lead rider because you cut through the wind and the rider behind gets the advantage of the slip stream which uses a little less effort, but I was feeling great and pushed hard keeping the pace up as much as was I was able to on the rough shoulder.

Arriving in Bordertown we were surprised to see so many people. Everywhere else we had been so quiet. There had been a flood of people rushing over the border this morning and it seemed that they were all hungry. We even had to line up in the bakery to be served.

Sitting outside on the grass eating our lunch we were approached by some people who gave us a donation for LHF and were interested to hear about my ride so far. This was what we had hoped to do the whole time, but COVID had changed that and although our online fundraising was still increasing slowly, we had not been able to talk to many people and get donations. We had hardly seen anyone to speak to.

After lunch we checked into our motel and then rode out to Mundulla to the farm Pop grew up on, passing the Mundulla Primary School where we were meant to speak at an assembly. Pop was very disappointed to have to miss that. After a quick visit to the farm, we rode back to Bordertown and enjoyed a takeaway meal while discussing what to do now that we could continue.

Pop and Peter gave the bikes a check and a clean as they did every night to make sure everything was working well for the next day. Peter then wheeled the bikes away for safe keeping overnight to his room.

Once again, the map came out. Could we somehow make up the kilometres that we had travelled in the car now that we were back in South Australia? It certainly would be possible, but still with daily press conferences and the unknown surrounding rumours of lockdowns and the growing problems of essential supplies in the shops, as well as my brother and sister in Adelaide with family, it was decided we needed to just head for Adelaide directly.

After the plan was set for the next day, Peter went for a walk to the roadhouse to get a coffee and was surprised to see that the border check point was not actually at the border but on the Adelaide side of Bordertown, 20 km from the border and directly in our route for the morning.

118 km 4 hours 27 minutes Average 26.6 km/h

A LITTLE BOY'S BIG DREAM

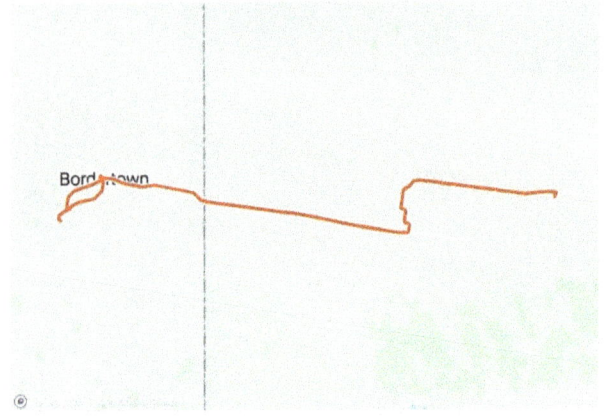

Distance
118.36 km

Elevation Gain
518 m

Moving Time
4:27:06

Avg Speed
26.6 km/h

Max Elevation
213 m

Max Speed
47.2 km/h

Leaving Nhill heading for the border

Chapter 11
Day Four

Wednesday 25th of March 2020
Bordertown – Coonalpyn

It was a chilly start again to the morning and I was feeling great that we were still riding. Pop had a plan to avoid the highway and the checkpoint because we were a little unsure about crossing through it today as we had already passed through yesterday.

Pop said, "Forget the plan and follow me. I will take you the backway so we can avoid the highway," So, with Pop leading and all the cars following, we made our way through town and when we reached the highway at Wirriga, the crew passed us and made their way to Keith to wait for us.

It was only a few minutes on the highway when we pulled over to speak to Peter.

Pop said, "It is terrible riding on the shoulder. It is far too rough and not very wide. We can feel every bump through our whole body, and it is exhausting."

After thinking about it for a few moments Peter said, "Ride on the road. I will signal with two honks of my horn to get off the road and onto the shoulder when a vehicle is coming. One honk will let you know when it is safe to get back on the road."

We got back on our bikes listening for Peter's signal. It worked well and was much easier to ride on the road as it was much smoother. Luckily there was not much traffic, mainly trucks and we were flying along, but even though we were on the shoulder each time a truck passed, there was a thundering noise and I had to hold tight to keep my line with the strong draft of the truck trying to push me sideways.

We made it to Keith at a good pace and sat out the front of the bakery enjoying a sausage roll and hot chocolate sitting on our camp chairs. I have travelled around South Australia a fair bit and tried many sausage rolls, and by far the best one I have ever had was that one in Keith!

Continuing towards Tintinara we kept up the signals and spent most of the way on the road listening for Peter's signal. If a vehicle was coming from behind, we trusted that Peter could be always aware, and we would be safe. Still filled with excitement that we had been allowed to continue riding I was feeling great, and my legs were working hard like it was the first day all over again, without the hills though!

Our lunch stop in the park at Tintinara was peaceful with hardly any traffic passing, it was rare now to see a car at all. On towards our final stop for the day in Coonalpyn and still feeling strong, the crew packed up and passed us a few kilometres down the road. We felt that we could have kept riding when we arrived in Coonalpyn. The crew was, as always, waiting to cheer for us as we arrived, but there really is nowhere to stay between Coonalpyn and Tailem Bend, and the owners of the hotel had been expecting us and even had given us the rooms at no cost.

The hotel, like all hotels and restaurants, had been forced to close. We were only able to enter via the back door into our rooms. Although the restaurant was closed, the owners kindly offered to cook us a meal. We had to sit out the back and eat on an old wooden table in the cold as we celebrated another great ride.

That day's ride was the fastest 100 km we had done so far. Each day we rode hard, conscious that Peter behind us was working hard to keep far enough behind us so that he didn't accidently hit us while also having to look behind for approaching vehicles, so we were pushing to ride as fast as we could the whole time.

It was at this time every day that I enjoyed reading messages of support and encouragement on my social media and checking my fundraising page. But over the last few days the messages and fundraising had begun to dry up. It was disappointing, and we were beginning to feel that people thought we should have given up and gone home.

To get my mind off all that was going on, I enjoyed kicking the footy around the backyard with Pop for a while until it got dark, and we had to go inside. We went to bed to make sure we were ready for what the next day would bring.

117 km 3 hours 59 minutes Average 29.3 km/h

RILEY'S BIG RIDE

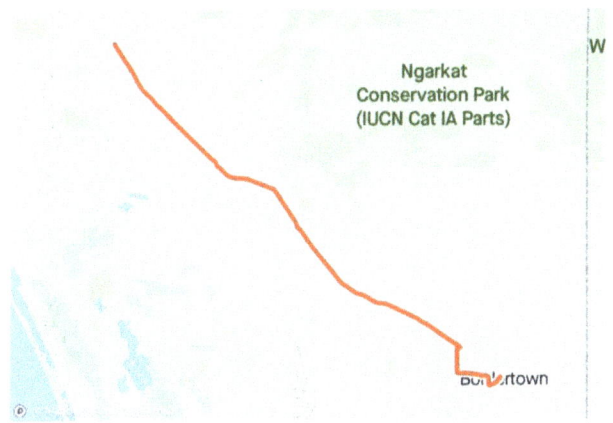

Distance
117.26 km

Elevation Gain
113 m

Moving Time
3:59:55

Avg Speed
29.3 km/h

Max Elevation
91 m

Max Speed
44.6 km/h

Mum and me in Keith, SA

Mum and Dad waiting for us to arrive in Coonalpyn

Chapter 12
Day Five

Thursday 26th of March 2020
Coonalpyn – Nairne

We were up early, and after a quick breakfast we were back on the highway. It was a very cold morning again, and we planned our first stop in Coomandook. With Peter still signalling us to get off the road for other traffic, we were going along well, but I didn't know that Pop was having trouble with his knee.

We met the crew in Coomandook where they had set up a nice morning tea for us. Although we were running short of food supplies, it was getting difficult to resupply now because some of the shops had signs saying that nonlocals were not welcome. People had been travelling from the city and buying up items in small towns. This meant that the locals were feeling angry that they were now unable to get essentials, so we were careful to keep our purchases to a minimum.

Pop said, "I have a terrible pain in my right knee." After taking some pain killers, he said, "I need to keep moving before I cool down too much." So, we left, heading towards Tailem Bend where we would stop for a lunch break.

It was my turn to take the lead and give Pop a rest in my slip stream. I worked hard to keep a good speed, listening carefully for Peter's signal to get off the road to avoid the traffic coming from behind. As we rode into Tailem Bend, I could see my banner hanging up next to the big rhino statue with the crew waving and cheering spurring me on as we continued into town.

The COVID rules had been changing daily, sometimes multiple times during the day, and the crew were working hard to keep up with them, making sure we were always compliant. Now only three people could go into the bakery at a time, so we waited until it was our turn and Mum went in and got our lunch. While I was, as always, enjoying my lunch, Peter suggested that instead of ending in Kanmantoo that we could extend the day's ride to end in Nairne to get some of the hills out of the way and make tomorrow easier for Pop's sore knee. We had the last bit of the highway to tackle and the only good thing about COVID was the lack of traffic. With Peter keeping us safe, we made it to Murray Bridge.

Getting off the highway was a relief for all of us. The road and shoulder the last few days since we had entered South Australia had not been good to ride on at all, and it had been difficult for Peter having to concentrate so much to keep us safe.

When we reached Murray Bridge it was fun going over the bridge as there was no space for anyone to overtake us and the speed limit was only 40 km/h. We raced across, not wanting to slow the cars down at all. We had a quick stop at a park where Pop spent some time laying on a park bench, and although he was still having pain in his knee, we decided that we would end today in Nairne. I was feeling great, so was happy to continue.

After the last couple of days with flat and at times boring roads we were now ready to start the ups and downs and bends of the Adelaide Hills. We made our way to Kanmantoo for a quick break, and then on to Nairne. I pushed up the hills and enjoyed the down sections, reminding me of how hard I find hills, but I was as determined as ever. Pop and I pushed hard, and when we arrived in Nairne we wondered if we should just finish today, but we decided that because a few people wanted to see us finish, we would pack up for the day. Driving home for the night to Nan and Pop's house we were feeling ready for a big finish tomorrow knowing that it wouldn't be the big celebration we had planned.

131 km 5 hours 12 minutes Average 25.2 km/h

Distance **131.17 km**	Elevation Gain **1,007 m**
Moving Time **5:12:14**	Avg Speed **25.2 km/h**
Max Elevation **393 m**	Max Speed **56.2 km/h**

Enjoying a break in Tintinara

Arriving in Murray Bridge

Pop resting his sore knee

Chapter 13
Day six
Friday 27th of March 2020
Nairne – Adelaide Oval

Driving back to Nairne to meet Peter and complete our ride to Adelaide Oval I was feeling excited and a little sad all at the same time. I remembered that we had to drive part of the way to meet Government requirements to cross the border before the deadline. The big celebration that we had planned was no longer possible. I realised that today would be the end of my big dream and it would all be over soon.

We arrived to find Peter waiting and ready to go, along with my Aunty Meg who had come to see us leave and wish us luck. My heart was beating at what seemed like a million miles an hour as we mounted our bikes and made our way through Littlehampton and Balhannah, where it was great to have someone waiting to cheer us on.

The next few kilometres were tough with some challenging hills. We found that we needed to use our lowest gear, but today the hills didn't bother me. I was ready for any challenge to get me over the finish line! We reached Uraidla where Mum and Dad were waiting with some morning tea. As this was where our now cancelled Police escort was to begin, Pop had organised our friends Wayne and John to meet us with their motorbikes to lead us the rest of the way to the city.

With the motorbikes in front and Peter behind us with lights flashing I felt proud that we had made it all this way. We began our final section and made our way down Old Norton Summit Road, hands squeezing the brakes so that we could control our speed on the steep descent, making sure to avoid an accident now that we had come so far.

It felt like we were flying along Magill Road and then as we rode along the River Torrens, I called out to Pop, "Look! I can see the Adelaide Oval." My heart was beating so hard with excitement I could hardly believe that the dream Pop and I had shared was about to come true.

I didn't know who would be there or if there would be anyone at all to celebrate. I also didn't know that Mum had hung our banner and drawn a chalk line to mark our end on the Plaza at the entrance to the Oval.

While setting up for our finish a security guard had come out of his office and said to Mum, "What are you doing? You can't gather here, please leave."

Mum answered with a firm "No. I am waiting to celebrate with my son!" There was no way Mum was leaving and the security guard realised that he was not going to change Mum's mind, so he gave up and went back to his office.

At this stage of the COVID rules it was illegal to have more than ten people gathered. With my parents, brother and sister, Nan, Gran and Pa waiting, and a few other friends and family spread out across the road, when we turned into the Plaza the cheers erupted so loud you would have thought there were 100 people cheering as Mum directed us to cross the line.

"We did it!" said Pop as we got off our bikes and gave each other a high five in celebration, forgetting for a moment all the disappointments created along the way by COVID-19.

42 km 1 hour 47 minutes Average 23.7 km/h

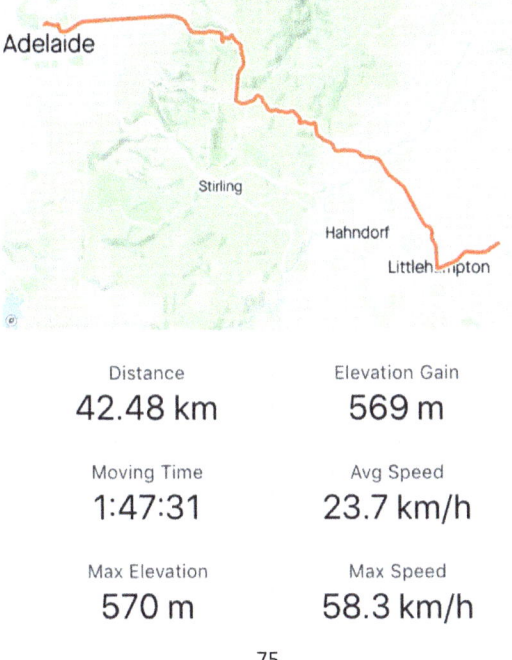

Leaving Nairne

Ready for the last leg

Adelaide Oval – we did it!

Our Trip:

Sunday March 22
Day 1 Melbourne (Docklands) to Ballarat 112 km

Monday March 23
Day 2 Ballarat to Stawell (Nhill) 130.5 km

Tuesday March 24
Day 3 Nhill to Bordertown 118 km

Wednesday March 25
Day 4 Bordertown to Coonalpyn 117 km

Thursday March 26
Day 5 Coonalpyn to Nairne 131 km

Friday March 27
Day 6 Nairne to Adelaide Oval 42.5 km

Total 651 kms

Peter and me

Pop's legs had never really recovered from the cramps he suffered on day one and he had pushed through a painful knee for a few days, but like me, he would never have thought to give up. My dream had also become Pop's dream. We were a great team encouraging each other when it was needed and always pushing each other to reach our goal.

651 km of riding in 25 hours and 6 minutes at an average of 26 km/h, not one flat tyre or breakdown, with the help of the crew, the protection of Peter in his Ute and prayers for our safety from many people we were finally home, and it was over.

We had planned a big dinner with family and friends to celebrate, but restaurants were closed, so we gathered at Nan and Pop's house with my family and Gran and Pa. We had takeaway pizza while we talked about our week, the challenges, and the achievements. It was a great celebration even though we were disappointed that circumstances didn't allow the celebration we had planned.

Nan went inside and, much to my surprise, presented me with a big box that had arrived from my friends at Bianchi Australia. Opening the box, I was excited to find some jerseys, helmets, hats and saddle bags. The support I had received from Bianchi was amazing and it was a special end to a very special day.

You can train hard and plan for everything, but some things are out of your control, so you need to learn how to adjust. We often said if only we had started our ride a day or even a week earlier how different it would have been. But, of course, it is not possible to change the past.

Chapter 14
Life Goes On

We were home after our epic adventure, but life was far from normal. Schools were closed in favour of home learning for a few weeks which meant that Mum had to stay home from work for a while and attempt to teach us. At times, we were not very cooperative!

Like many others, Pop had to work from home. If Mum needed to go to the supermarket, she had to wait for Dad to get home because only one person from the household could go at a time and everything seemed so strange.

Would life ever be normal again?

While all of this was going on I was feeling as though I had not achieved my goals. The first thing I decided to correct was my fundraising for the Little Heroes Foundation. I was so close to the $8000 goal I had set and only about $500 to go.

Nan had the idea of asking people via our social media to set challenges, and for a donation, Pop and I would complete them. I was thrilled when someone set us a challenge to ride 100 km in less than 4 hours. I thought that it was an easy challenge, but as always, I was determined to get it done. The next weekend we were off for a ride down towards the coast and reached the 100 km mark in 3 hours and 38 minutes. Deciding that 100 km wasn't enough, we continued the ride and when we reached home had clocked up 161 km.

It was great to see the fundraising total moving again and the next weekend another challenge was set to ride from home to Clare. So, in high spirits and the hope that this would bring our total raised to our goal, we left early and reached Clare in time for lunch. While we were eating, Pop called Nan to tell her that we had reached Clare but that we would continue to Auburn and could she come and pick us up. Another 160 km that day and our fundraising goal was achieved, with a total of $8333 going to the Little Heroes Foundation. I felt satisfied that I had been able to reach that goal because it was very important to me.

Now that the fundraising was taken care of there was still the feeling I could do more. Pop and I were still riding most weekends, although we had to choose our routes a little differently because it had become difficult to find places for lunch in some areas. We were still enjoying our riding and our fitness was still as good as when we left Melbourne.

The football season had been suspended, so riding was a way for me to keep busy on Saturdays. We had completed our 2nd 200 km one weekend, and I was trying to think what I could do to make up for missing those kilometres when we had to cross the border.

"How far do you think we can ride in one day?" Pop asked me as we were riding along one day. I wasn't sure, but I knew that I could ride 200 km. We had done that twice, but how far could I go was now on my mind.

That was when I decided to contact Illia my old school principal, who is a cyclist and had been so encouraging during my training. I asked him what his longest ride was. 230 km he told me. That was it.

"I will beat that before my 9th birthday," I said to Pop with confidence and determination. I was excited to have a new challenge to complete.

With the sun still not up and the temperature only three degrees just before 6.30 am in July of 2020, and just one month before my 9th birthday, with Peter once again in his big red Ute, lights flashing behind, we set of for what would be an epic day of riding.

The sun slowly came up as we passed through Two Wells, but our fingers and toes were still frozen when we reached Balaklava to have our first decent break.

There wasn't much traffic around that morning as we headed toward the parking bay at the top of the York Highway just past Port Wakefield where we met Mum and Nan who had a nice morning tea waiting for us. 98 km had already been done and we were feeling great. It had warmed up a bit by now and we had a slight tail wind behind us helping along.

We kept riding and arrived in Ardrossan to meet Mum and Nan for lunch. We now had just a little over 100 km to go and were still feeling strong. When we left heading towards Minlaton and we were just a few kilometres down the road, Pop got a flat tyre! We stopped on the side of the road the tube was quickly changed.

It was great to have Peter behind as the traffic had gotten heavier. The road was not very wide in some places and the motorists were quite impatient at times. As we turned off the road to head to Minlaton we began climbing up and the ride became a little more challenging, so I found myself pushing hard to keep up with Pop and was glad to arrive for a break and have something to eat.

The day was nearly done with just about 50 km to go. I was keen to keep going even though I was feeling a bit tired; Pop and I take a challenge very seriously so was excited to finish this one. As we rode past Stansbury, Mum and Nan were at the corner cheering us on just 23 km to go.

The sun was beginning to set as we were getting closer to Edithburgh and the air was getting colder although there was hardly any wind. My legs were feeling tired, but I kept pushing. We would be done soon I told myself.

Mum and Nan would be waiting for us at the jetty. Pop had studied the map carefully before we left so that our distance would be just right. We entered the town in the dark and made our way to the jetty where we spotted Mum and Nan standing in the dark feeling very cold but ready to meet us. It was just before 6 pm. I jumped off my bike and lifted it up as high as I could to celebrate, while Pop struggled to get off his bike and sat down so Nan could remove his shoes.

Feeling hungry we set off to find something to eat before driving home. All the restaurants were full because of the capacity rules, so we got some takeaway and had to sit outside on the footpath in the cold and eat. COVID was once again making life hard, but I was thrilled to have achieved my goal for the day.

I was cold and tired so when we got in the car, I wrapped myself up in a blanket and slept all the way home.

240.8 kms 9 hours 30 minutes Average 25.3 km/h

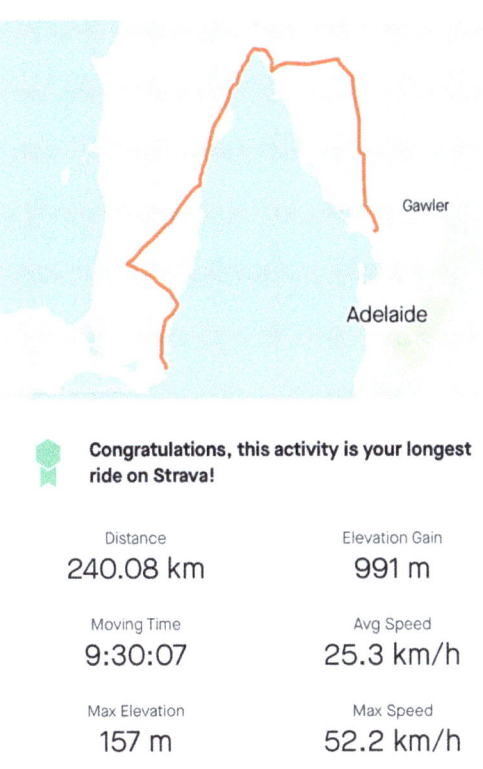

Congratulations, this activity is your longest ride on Strava!

Distance
240.08 km

Elevation Gain
991 m

Moving Time
9:30:07

Avg Speed
25.3 km/h

Max Elevation
157 m

Max Speed
52.2 km/h

Enjoying a break

Dreams can be big or small but some dreams, especially one like mine, are not possible to do alone. I am thankful to those who helped me achieve my dream. Young or old, if you have a dream and decide to give it a go, work hard and don't give up -- your dreams can come true!

DO YOU HAVE A DREAM?

Chapter 15
Riley Now

It's been over 5 years since my big adventure.

When Pop and I returned from Melbourne, we were invited to join the Port Adelaide Cycling Club. We spent about 18 months enjoying track cycling and I also participated in some time trials. It was great fun, and we met some interesting people who taught us a lot.

Being invited to join the Bianchi Owners Club Australia was another great opportunity. Pop and I went back to Melbourne to participate in their yearly ride and met some of my followers. We enjoyed the ride and loved being able to ride in a large group.

We also rode in a charity ride raising money for Breakthrough Mental Health, a 100 km ride hosted by Erin Phillips and Mark Soderstrom. It was a tough ride from the city up through the Hills and back.

I have since grown out of my cycling gear and shoes and then grew out of Pop's gear. My bike is also far too small for me, so it's been a while since I have been riding.

My interests are a bit different now. I am in High School. My favourite subjects are PE, home economics and agriculture. On the weekends I love playing football, going to Church with my family and hanging out with my mates. Sometimes we camp out in our swags and cook on a campfire or ride motorbikes.

I still enjoy time with my Pop, even if we don't spend as much time together as we used to. But each night, when I go to bed, I see my framed jersey on the wall. And I remember our big adventure. I remember that—with hard work, determination, and support—dreams can come true.

My framed jersey

From the author

My dream was to write this book for Riley.
Here it is at last; I hope you like it buddy.

I could not have written this book without support from my family. Thank you, Paul, Amy, and Kelly for your encouragement and suggestions. Joel, thank you for telling me when my words were rubbish and making me throw them away even when it made me cross.

Riley, without the dream you shared with Pop, I wouldn't have had a great story to write. Your determination, hard work and ability to keep going even when things got tough—and at times it was very tough—amazed me and made me proud beyond words.

My hope is that all our grandchildren—not only Riley but also Toby, Dakota, Daisy, Hartley, Henry, and Lucas—will be inspired to follow their dreams, whatever they may be!

Love Sandy – Mum – Nan.

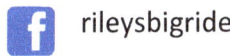 rileysbigride

www.rileysbigride.home.blog

For more information or to order
copies of this book:
Email Sandy Turnbull
psturnbull86@gmail.com

For schoolteachers download resources:
www.tinyurl.com/3ev7sspj
Resources thanks to Joel Turnbull.

To learn more or to support
The Little Heroes Foundation
www.littleheroesfoundation.com.au

www.megshepherddesigns.com.au

www.ingramcontent.com/pod-product-compliance
Lightning Source LLC
Chambersburg PA
CBHW062040290426
44109CB00026B/2690